Contents

The story so far

If you haven't read an *On the edge* book before:
The stories take place in and around a row of shops and buildings called Pier Parade in Brightsea, right next to the sea. There's Big Fry, the fish and chip shop; Drop Zone, the drop-in centre for local teenagers; Macmillan's, the sweet and souvenir shop; Anglers' Haven, the fishing tackle shop; the Surf 'n' Skate shop and, of course, the Brightsea Beach Bar (the 3Bs).

If you have read an *On the edge* book you may have met some of these people before.

Owen Robbins:	*new to his school, Owen is in a wheelchair and can't walk.*
Adil Hussain:	*another boy in the same class. His father, Rafiq, drives Owen to school in a taxi.*

So, what's been going on?
Owen is in a wheelchair, but wants to lead an active life. However, his mother wants to protect him and worries that he'll get hurt at school.

What happens in this story?
Owen asks his mum if he can go to the school disco but she says he can't. So, Owen works out a plan with the help of new friend Adil. The thing is, mums are smart, and just when he thinks he's fooled her, Owen's mum does some checking up…

1

Fed up

Owen Robbins sat in his wheelchair.

He was in the kitchen.

He looked fed up.

"You're not going, and that's it!" said his mum.

Owen looked at her.

"Why not? Everyone's going," he said.

Owen was talking about the school disco.

It was going to take place on Friday.

His mum sighed.

"It's not safe!" she said.

She pushed Owen towards the table.

"I'm not hungry!" he said.

"Of course you are. I've done your favourite."

Owen felt hungry really.

But he was cross.

Owen felt hungry really.
But he was cross.

Too cross to eat.

His mum put a plate on the table.

It was pasta and meatballs.

Owen looked at the plate.

It did look nice.

"All right. I'll have some, but I'm *not*

hungry!" he said.

His mum sat down.

"Why can't I go?" asked Owen.

His mum put down her knife and fork.

"Suppose you fell out of your

wheelchair?" she said.

"Someone would help me," he replied.

"Who?" his mum asked. "You have only just started at the school."

"I don't need anyone!" said Owen.

He pushed his plate away.

"I'm not a cripple!" he shouted.

2

Plans

Owen wheeled himself up the slope.

The school had slopes for wheelchairs.

Sometimes he needed help.

Most of the time he did it himself.

He had strong arms.

Today, he felt tired.

"Hi, Owen," said a teacher. "Do you need a hand?"

"No – I need a pair of legs!" said Owen.

The teacher didn't know whether to laugh or not.

"It's a joke!" said Owen.

The teacher smiled.

It was Mr Briggs.

Owen's form teacher.

Mr Briggs held the door of the classroom open.

Owen went in.

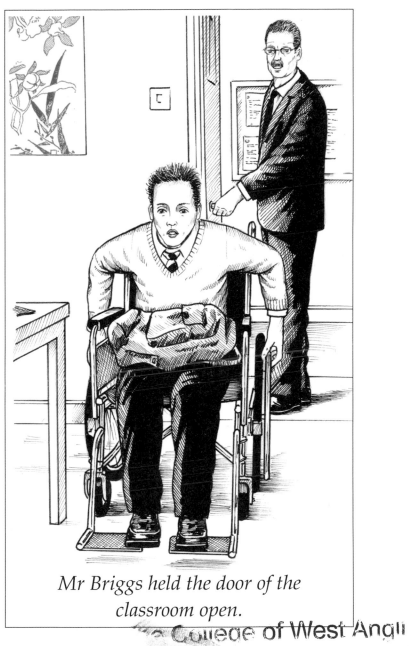

Mr Briggs held the door of the classroom open.

13

"Thanks, sir," he said.

Most of the class were there.

They were in groups, talking.

It was the start of the school day.

One or two said "Hi" to Owen.

Then they went back to their friends.

Owen wheeled himself to one side.

He started thinking.

He had to go to this disco.

How else would he meet people?

One or two said "Hi" to Owen.
Then they went back to their friends.

He got the letter about the disco out of his bag.

He tore off the reply slip.

He filled in his own name in his mum's writing.

Then he signed her name.

3

TGIF

"Thank God it's Friday!" said Owen's mum.

It was breakfast time.

Owen's mum worked in the town centre.

It was close to Christmas so all the shops were busy.

"I might be a bit late tonight," she said.

"The taxi driver will drop you off. He can open the front door too."

Owen frowned.

"I don't need him to help me!" he said.

"OK. If you say so," his mum replied.

She hurried out into the hall.

Then she called out to him.

"Owen! Your taxi's here!"

Owen ate the last bit of toast.

Then he wheeled himself out into the hall.

He grabbed his coat.

The taxi driver was waiting.

"All right, Owen?" he said.

Owen liked Rafiq, the taxi driver.

He treated him normally.

Rafiq helped Owen into the taxi.

"You going to this disco, then?" asked Rafiq. "Might be some nice girls there!"

"My mum won't let me!" said Owen. "She says it will be too dangerous."

"But you have to go to the school disco!" said Rafiq.

"That's what I said," replied Owen.

"Do you know my son, Adil?" asked Rafiq.

"Yes – he's in my class."

"It's funny. He doesn't want to go!"

Rafiq started the car, and they set off for school.

4

Helping out

At school, Adil was sitting on his own.

Owen wheeled himself over.

"I know your dad," said Owen.

"I know," said Adil. "He's your taxi driver."

"He's OK," said Owen.

"No he's not. He's trying to make me go to this stupid disco!"

Adil looked fed up.

"Don't you want to go?"

"Course not. It's stupid!" said Adil.

Owen thought hard.

Adil often sat on his own.

Perhaps Adil wanted to go but didn't have any friends.

"I'm going!" said Owen.

"Are you?" asked Adil.

"Yeah, but I need someone to help me down the steps."

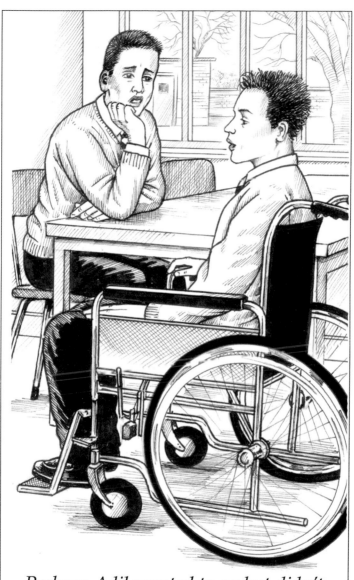

Perhaps Adil wanted to go but didn't have any friends.

Adil thought about it.

He did want to go to the disco really.

"I could help you!" said Adil.

"I need your help in another way, too," said Owen.

"Sure," said Adil. "Whatever you say!"

"Can I come back to your house for tea? Then we could go to the disco together."

Adil thought about it.

Why not?

His dad knew Owen.

"Sure!" said Adil.

'Sure' was Adil's favourite word.

"Cool!" said Owen. "I've got my clothes in my bag."

Owen was happy.

Part one of the plan had worked.

Now for the tricky bit!

5

Not really a lie

"Hi, Mum!" said Owen into the phone.

He was at Adil's house.

His mum was on her mobile.

"Hi, Owen," she said.

"Is it all right if I stay for tea at Adil's

tonight?" he asked.

"Is that Rafiq's son?" asked his mum.

"Yes. He's in my class. He's my best mate."

Owen winked at Adil.

"I suppose so," she said. "Shall I pick you up?"

"No – it's OK. Adil's dad will bring me back."

His mum thought about speaking to Rafiq.

But she knew him.

He was the taxi driver and seemed very nice.

"OK. See you later!" said his mum.

Owen smiled at Adil.

"Disco, here we come!" said Owen.

At the disco, Owen showed what he could do.

He did some really flashy moves in his wheelchair.

In one of them he spun to the right.

Then he spun to the left.

Next he rocked back so the front wheels left the ground.

All the kids from the school clapped.

At the disco, Owen showed what
he could do.

Adil thought it was great, too.

He'd made some new friends.

But it was almost time to go home.

Parents were waiting at the door.

Then Owen saw her.

His mum.

She walked across the floor.

She looked really cross.

"You lied to me!" she said.

"How did you find out?" asked Owen.

"I decided to phone Adil's dad after all," she said.

"You can't protect me all my life, mum!" said Owen.

His mum sighed.

She looked at Owen and his new friends.

The last song began.

It was a fast song.

"Let me stay for this last one. Please," said Owen.

A girl came over.

"Coming, Owen?" she asked.

His mum looked around.

Everyone was dancing and singing.

"Go on," she said, smiling. "Just watch you don't run anyone over!"

Glossary

course not	of course not
cripple	unpleasant term used to describe a disabled person
(to) drop (someone) off	(to) use the car to take someone somewhere, then leave them there
fed up	unhappy
flashy	showy, likely to impress
(to) frown	(to) make a face to show anger
funny	odd
mate	friend
(to) pick (someone) up	(to) collect someone by car
reply slip	paper at the bottom of a letter on which a reply is written
(to) sign one's name	(to) write one's name in a particular style
smart	clever
(to) spin	(to) move round quickly in a circle
TGIF	abbreviation for 'Thank God It's Friday'
tricky	difficult, needing a special skill